D1686044

THIS NOTEBOOK BELONGS TO.............................................................

CONTACT.............................................................

See our range of fine, illustrated books, ebooks, notebooks and art calendars:
**www.flametreepublishing.com**

This is a **FLAME TREE NOTEBOOK**
Published and © copyright 2019 Flame Tree Publishing Ltd

FTPB86 • 978-1-78755-581-5

# MOOMIN

Cover image based on a detail from
*Moomin Love* by Tove Jansson (1914–2001)
© Moomin Characters™

Tove Jansson was a Finnish-Swedish writer and artist who created the Moomin family
and their friends. She first started painting Moomintrolls in 1935 and her last Moomin
book was published in 1970; but her stories live on and continue to be adapted and
enjoyed by many generations.

**FLAME TREE PUBLISHING** | The Art of Fine Gifts
6 Melbray Mews, London SW6 3NS, United Kingdom